This is a fictionalised biography describing some of the key moments (so far!) in the career of Marcus Rashford.

Some of the events described in this book are based upon the author's imagination and are probably not entirely accurate representations of what actually happened.

Tales from the Pitch
Marcus Rashford
by Harry Coninx

Published in the United State of America and Canada
by Leapfrog Press
www.leapfrogpress.com

Distributed in the United States by
Consortium Book Sales and Distribution
St Paul, Minnesota 55114
www.cbsd.com

First Published in the United Kingdom by Raven Books
An imprint of Ransom Publishing Ltd.
Unit 7, Brocklands Farm, West Meon, Hampshire GU32 1JN, UK
www.ransom.co.uk

ISBN 978-1-948585-83-5
Also available as an eBook
First published in the United States 2023

TALES FROM THE PITCH

MARCUS RASHFORD

HARRY CONINX

Leapfrog Press
New York and London

For my sister Georgia, who spent a lot of time in goal
so that I could practice my shooting

CONTENTS

I

THE COOLEST MAN IN THE STADIUM

March 2019, Parc des Princes, Paris, France
PSG v Manchester United

As Marcus looked around at the players who were sitting in the Manchester United dressing room, he couldn't fail to see that many of his usual team-mates were missing.

There was no Paul Pogba, no Alexis Sánchez, no Anthony Martial, no Juan Mata, no Jesse Lingard, no Phil Jones, no Ander Herrera and no Nemanja Matic

"You could almost make a starting eleven out of all the players who're injured or suspended," Romelu Lukaku muttered next to him, following his gaze.

Marcus smiled at the Belgian striker, who'd only just come back from injury himself.

"This could be a long night," he said quietly, "but I think we can do it."

The nervous atmosphere in the Man United dressing room suggested that few of his team-mates felt the same way.

United had taken on PSG at Old Trafford two weeks earlier, in the first leg of this Champions League Last 16 tie, and they'd been comfortably beaten 2-0.

"If we couldn't beat them at home, how on earth are we going to beat them here?" Andreas Pereira asked, voicing the one question that had been hanging over the whole team ever since that defeat.

Marcus turned to Man United's new manager, Ole Gunnar Solskjær, thinking that he would reassure the youngster. But Ole was busy talking with his coaching assistants and hadn't heard Andreas.

So Marcus stood up to look for one of the senior

players, to ask them to give Andreas some reassurance.

But then it occurred to him. Marcus was only twenty-one, but he was more experienced than most of the players in the squad tonight. *He* could set an example and inspire the team.

"We weren't thrashed, Andreas," Marcus said clearly and loudly, ensuring that everyone could hear. "It was nil-nil for most of that game – we just need an early goal tonight. We get that, then they'll start to panic – and that's when we have to take advantage."

Team captain Ashley Young nodded in agreement. "We have to take risks today, lads," he said, signalling for everyone to get to their feet. "We have nothing to lose tonight."

Barely moments later, Marcus found himself standing out in the rain, listening to the familiar anthem draw to a close.

Taking a deep breath, he started working his way down the line of PSG players, shaking the hands of Kylian Mbappé, Ángel Di María, Julian Draxler, Thiago Silva ... the line of superstars seemed endless.

Each of these players oozed confidence, but within

two minutes of the starting whistle, everything had changed.

A sloppy back-pass by Thilo Kehrer was intercepted by Man United's Lukaku and the striker pounced, racing around PSG keeper Gianluigi Buffon before sliding the ball into the net.

United had the early goal they needed.

"Come on, Rom!" Marcus yelled, gesturing for the striker to come back to the half-way line. "We still need another two!"

Just as Marcus had told the team in the dressing room, Man United didn't want PSG thinking clearly. They needed to strike now, while the French team were panicking and making mistakes.

But 10 minutes later, PSG's quality showed. Kylian Mbappé got in behind and whipped the ball across the goal. Juan Bernat was waiting at the back post and he tapped it in.

United still only needed two goals to go through, but now, back at 1-1, PSG had their tails up.

Luckily for Man United the wet pitch was causing havoc for PSG's defenders – and every time they slipped

Marcus was able to get in behind them. But he was failing to capitalise on the opportunities.

"Marcus!" Ashley Young called over to him. "Have a shot. When it's this wet, if it bounces it's going to go all over the place."

Marcus nodded and a few minutes later he got his chance, picking up the ball and fizzing a shot towards goal.

It wasn't his best effort, but it skidded along the wet grass and Buffon failed to hold on to it. Lukaku was ready to pounce and he tucked in the rebound.

Now United were leading 2-1, but they were still behind on aggregate.

"We need one more, boys!" Marcus roared. "Just one more and we go through on away goals!"

But the goal wasn't coming.

As the second half played out, PSG were dominant. Mbappé had chances, Di María had chances ... but time and time again, through a combination of luck and good defending, United held firm.

Marcus looked over to the bench, almost willing Pogba or Martial to appear magically to help rescue the game.

It wasn't to be, although manager Ole did send on Diogo Dalot and Tahith Chong, two players who were both still teenagers.

But when the game got back underway it was Dalot who made the difference. In the last minutes of the game he picked the ball up about 25 yards out and fired it towards goal. It deflected off a PSG defender and flew out for a corner.

"Come on!" Marcus bellowed, calling for United's defenders to come up – but the ref had stopped play.

"What's going on?" Luke Shaw asked, coming up behind Marcus.

"I don't know," he replied.

"It was handball!" Dalot shouted, shoving his way past some of the PSG players. "I'm telling you, it was handball."

The ref indicated that he was going to check the VAR screen, and then he jogged over to the touchline.

The whole stadium held its breath and Marcus looked at the scoreboard.

They were in the 89th minute. If a penalty was given, United would have the chance to do the impossible.

After what seemed like hours of deliberation, the ref finally marched back onto the pitch and pointed at the penalty spot.

While all the United players and fans roared in celebration, and all the PSG players and fans shrieked their protests, Marcus simply walked over and picked up the ball.

This was going to be his first professional penalty for United.

The PSG players were swirling about in front of him, arguing with the referee, gesticulating wildly, but Marcus ignored them.

There was only one thought in his mind, and he couldn't allow himself to overthink it.

Eventually, after all the commotion had subsided, he was able to step up, even though out of the corner of his eye he could still see some of the PSG players clashing with his team-mates behind him.

Blocking them out, he took several steps back and just stared at Buffon, who was looming large in the goal. This legendary goalkeeper had been playing Champions League football before Marcus was even born.

The referee blew his whistle and Marcus side-stepped to the left, then ran forward. He met the ball sweetly and fizzed it towards the top-left corner …

GOAL!

It was 3-1 to United, 3-3 on aggregate – but United had the most away goals. They were through to the Champions League quarter-finals, under the most incredible, seemingly impossible circumstances!

Adrenaline surged through Marcus's body and he raced toward the corner flag, sliding across the wet turf in front of the United fans who'd made the trip to Paris.

He only had a second to see their euphoric faces before he was smothered by his team-mates.

"How'd you do it, Marcus?" Andreas Pereira shouted at him. "You were the coolest person in the stadium!"

Too giddy to speak, Marcus just laughed.

The truth was that he'd scored that penalty a thousand times already – each time as a little boy in his garden.

And when it came to stunning the world with game-changing goals, Marcus felt that he still had a lot more to give.

2
MADE IN MANCHESTER

April 2003, Old Trafford, Manchester, England
Manchester United v Real Madrid

Five-year-old Marcus tried to keep up with his older brother Dwaine as they raced to their seats – but he had to keep stopping and looking around him.

Marcus had grown up in a family – and a neighbourhood – that was obsessed with Manchester United, and he'd seen Old Trafford countless times on TV.

But nothing had quite prepared him for actually being in the ground itself.

"Welcome to the theatre of dreams, buddy," Dwaine murmured, before grabbing Marcus's arm and pulling him along.

"I just can't believe Mum let us come here tonight," Marcus said, as they walked down the steps and took their seats.

"She knows it's a big game," Dwaine replied. "You don't want your first time at Old Trafford to be a boring old 3-0 win against Aston Villa or something."

Marcus nodded, but he really didn't mind what game he saw. He was just excited to be inside his club's stadium for the first time. *This* was where titles had been won, where legends had been made – and you could feel it in the air.

"It's so … so *busy*," Marcus said, staring out over the seemingly endless sea of fans, all dressed in the red team colours of Man United.

"It *is* a Champions League quarter final against Real Madrid!" Dwaine scoffed. "What did you expect?"

Marcus instantly started rocking in his seat in

excitement. He didn't know very much about teams outside England, but he did know about Real Madrid. They had Raúl, Luís Figo, Zinedine Zidane and Brazilian striker Ronaldo – in other words, some of the biggest names in football.

It wasn't long before the famous chant was building within the crowd, signalling that the game was about to begin.

"ATTACK! ATTACK! ATTACK!"

"Remember," Dwaine shouted in Marcus's ear, "we're 3-1 down from the first leg. It's a big ask, but I reckon we might be able to do it."

Marcus nodded in agreement and moved forward, sitting on the edge of his seat. They hadn't been able to afford better seats nearer the pitch, so they didn't have a great view of the game.

As the game kicked-off Marcus had to squint to work out who was who, but it didn't make seeing his heroes kicking a ball in real life any less special.

In this electrifying atmosphere he was desperate to be down there with the Man United players, to be playing a pass or having a shot on the Old Trafford turf.

He couldn't imagine what it must be like for the Madrid players. Every poor pass or mistake was met with a cacophony of boos and jeers, but it certainly didn't stop their number 11, Ronaldo, breaking the deadlock.

The Brazilian striker fired a shot away from the edge of the box and it bounced past Barthez and into the United goal.

For a split-second, Marcus didn't know how to react. It was a sensational goal to witness, but it was against his team.

He decided to turn to Dwaine. There was no one whose opinion he trusted more when it came to football, and he wanted to see what his brother made of it.

"Blimey, did you see how early he took that shot?" Dwaine said, clearly just as impressed. "Barthez didn't have a chance to set himself. But don't worry, bro, it's not over yet."

He was right. United continued to attack the Madrid goal and just before half-time van Nistelrooy tapped in from a Solskjær cross to equalise.

Marcus automatically sprang to his feet, along with the rest of the crowd, but he hadn't actually been paying attention to his United heroes. Ever since that first goal, he hadn't been able to stop watching Madrid's Ronaldo. The Brazilian fascinated him – he was always in space, always looking for the ball.

Marcus was secretly delighted when Ronaldo soon got his name on the scoresheet for a second time.

Again, United managed pulled one back, but it wasn't enough. Ronaldo followed up with a third, a screamer from 30 yards out.

"We need a striker like him," Marcus shouted over the noise of the crowd, as he watched Ronaldo celebrate his hat-trick.

It appeared that everybody else in the stadium agreed, as when the Brazilian was subbed off 15 minutes later he was given a standing ovation by the crowd – including the United fans. They knew they'd just witnessed a world-class performance from a very special player.

Looking around the majestic stadium and seeing everyone on their feet applauding Ronaldo took Marcus's breath away, and at that moment he made an important decision.

As soon as he got home, he was going to practise his football harder than ever before – because, one day, he was going to be playing for this club in this very stadium.

And he wanted to be just as deadly a striker as Ronaldo.

3
FLETCHER MOSS RANGERS

May 2005, Mersey Bank playing fields, Manchester

"I'm telling you! That's a scout from Manchester United!"

Marcus looked over to where his team-mate Cameron was pointing and saw a group of men clustered together at the far end of the pitch, scribbling in notebooks.

His heart skipped a beat at the thought that someone

from Man United might be watching him playing in the tournament today, writing his name in one of those notebooks and then drawing a big circle around it.

It wouldn't be the first time that somebody from this youth club, Fletcher Moss Rangers, got themselves signed up to a big team. There were pictures of United defender Wes Brown all around the clubhouse.

Today was a tournament involving all the local youth clubs, so it was a good opportunity for scouts to get to see a lot of local players in a single day.

Marcus turned back to Cameron, who was busy listing all the clubs he thought the scouts were from.

"And Danny said he saw somebody from Liverpool, but I'm not sure. But there's definitely someone from Man City there."

"Ugh!" Marcus said, pretending to vomit. "There's no way I'd ever play for City – or for Liverpool!"

Marcus's loyalty to Man United was well known to his friends, so Cameron just rolled his eyes and pulled him toward their team's warm-up.

As Marcus got stuck in to their warm-up routine, he looked around fondly.

He'd been a part of Fletcher Moss Rangers for two years now, but he could still remember the day his mum had arranged for him to sign up with them, wanting to direct his love for football somewhere other than their home.

Marcus had been only five then, but he'd broken more lamps than he or his mum could count, and after watching the Champions League quarter-finals at Old Trafford, 'accidents' had been happening more and more frequently.

Even moving him outside into the garden hadn't helped. He'd cracked the wheelie bin by chipping balls into it, and he'd damaged the garage roof by kicking balls on to it so he could control them as they rolled back off.

"Right, Marcus," his mum had said eventually, "you need a proper pitch and some proper team-mates."

And that had led him here.

"It's time, boys," Dave Horrocks, the Fletcher Moss coach, suddenly shouted, bringing Marcus's thoughts back to the present. "Just remember what we've practised and leave everything out on the pitch!"

Rangers' first game of the tournament started off slowly, with striker Marcus seeing very little of the ball.

In fact he could only watch from the other end of the pitch as Rangers' opponents took the lead, then doubled it a few moments later.

Marcus kicked the ground in frustration.

He knew Dave wanted him to stay up front, close to the goal – but it clearly wasn't working, and he had to do something to help the team.

He thought of his hero, Ronaldo. Since seeing him play at Old Trafford, Marcus had watched countless videos of Ronaldo's highlights and goals on YouTube and he was struck by the fact that Ronaldo always moved so freely.

As the game recommenced, Marcus decided to do the same thing, dropping deep.

"Marcus!" Dave bellowed from the touchline, "stay where you are! Hold your position!"

Marcus felt bad, but he pretended not to hear his coach, and kept moving further down the pitch until his team-mates could safely get the ball to him.

As soon as he had possession he spun, flicking the

ball around an opposition defender, and then he started driving back towards goal.

When another defender came out to challenge him, he did a quick stepover and skipped past him. Now, looking up, he could see only the keeper.

The keeper had set himself in goal, but Marcus could sense that this player wasn't a natural goalkeeper – most likely he was a defender being played out of position, somebody who wouldn't want to dive.

With that in mind, Marcus fired the ball high into the top-right corner, and it whistled past the keeper who, sure enough, just flapped at it with his hands.

GOAL!

As his Fletcher Moss team-mates came sprinting over to celebrate with him, Marcus glanced over at Dave, hoping that he wasn't angry with him. Dave was a really supportive coach, and he always took the time to give Marcus a little extra advice at the end of each practice session, noticing that he wasn't finding the sessions all that challenging.

But now Dave was just shaking his head with a wry smile on his face. He was very fond of Marcus, even though he was often caught off guard by the fact that a seven-year-old could have such a natural awareness for the game.

Fletcher Moss remained dominant for the rest of the match, with Marcus adding three more goals to their total before the referee finally blew the whistle for full-time.

"You played well, Marcus," Dave said, clapping him on the back as they came off the pitch.

"Even though I moved out of position?" Marcus asked, a cheeky smile on his face.

"Yes, even then," Dave chuckled. "If you keep playing like that, you could be the next Wes Brown. There's a lot of scouts watching us."

Marcus's eyes lit up. He'd become so involved in the game that he'd completely forgotten about the scouts.

He kept up his form for the rest of the day, carrying Fletcher Moss Rangers all the way to the final, which they won 2-1.

Marcus knew he'd played well and, as he stood waiting for Dwaine to come and collect him at the end of the day, he was ready to be tapped on the shoulder by the Man United scout, maybe even handed a phone with Sir Alex Ferguson waiting on the other end of the line.

But, in the end, it was just Dwaine who came over to him.

"What's up with you?" Dwaine asked, noticing Marcus's look of disappointment. Dwaine had watched enough football to know that his little brother already had something about him, so he was sure he couldn't be upset at having played badly.

"Some scouts watched us play today," Marcus explained, as they started to walk to the bus stop. "I kind of thought the United one might want to make me an offer to join their academy, but he didn't."

"Don't be thick," Dwaine said, bumping shoulders with Marcus. "You've got to give them some time to go and talk to their bosses, who go and talk to *their* bosses … If they've seen you play, I reckon they'll be in touch."

4

APART FOR UNITED

November 2008, Marcus's childhood home, Manchester

Marcus fell in through the door after another day of training at the Manchester United Academy and slumped onto the sofa.

He'd been lying on this same sofa, in exactly the same position, on the day when his mum had come over with a huge smile on her face – having just received a call from Manchester United.

Dwaine had been right – a two-week wait was all it took for the Man United scout to speak to his bosses after the tournament.

That had been three years ago, and since then Marcus had been attending school in the daytime, then training at the academy straight afterwards.

For Marcus it was a dream come true, but it was also pretty exhausting, especially as the training at the academy was getting more and more intense each year. Although of course he wouldn't change any of it for the world.

Marcus had loved his time with Fletcher Moss Rangers, but he'd always been the best player on the pitch, which had made it hard for him to progress. Now the others at the academy played as well as, if not better than, him and he could feel himself improving as a result.

So feeling a bit tired at the end of each day was a small price to pay for being a part of this incredible club – a club that, in the years since he'd joined, had come to dominate the Premier League.

Marcus closed his eyes and started to picture himself lifting the trophy with the first team one day, looking out at a sea of fans – when he was suddenly shaken awake.

He opened his eyes to see his mum, Melanie, standing over him.

"Your homework," she said, glaring at him. "Now."

"But Mum," he complained, "I've just got in. And I'm hungry!"

"Tea will be ready in 30 minutes," she replied. "Your homework is ready for you right now."

Marcus groaned, then got up reluctantly and walked over to the kitchen table, picking up his school bag on the way. The bag was almost knocked out of his hand as his two older brothers rushed past him, each attempting to wrestle the other to the ground.

"Oi!" Marcus shouted, "I've got homework to do over here!"

"'Should have done it earlier," Dwaine shouted back.

"I was training," Marcus snapped. "I *am* at Man United, you know!"

"Oh shut up, Marcus!" Dwaine said, pulling him under his arm and rubbing his head. "You may be at United, but when you're in *this* house, you're not so special!"

As Marcus started to wriggle his way out of Dwaine's grasp, he couldn't help but smile. Some of the boys at the academy, such as his friend Matt, were already getting pretty stuck-up about the whole 'academy' thing. He didn't want to be like that – and with his brothers around he knew that wasn't likely to happen.

By the time Marcus had finally escaped Dwaine and had actually sat down to do his homework, his mum was already bringing his tea in.

Tea turned out to be the same meal as yesterday and Marcus automatically pulled a face.

"Don't give me that," his mum said, "money is a bit tight at the moment."

Marcus instantly felt guilty – and not just for making the face.

He was sure that all the bus tickets to get him to and from training were the main reason why things were tight at the moment, not to mention the amount of football kit he was getting through.

He hated the thought that he was putting a strain on his mum. She was already working so hard to give him and his brothers everything they needed.

Then a thought struck him.

"Mum, when you're twelve you can start a programme at the academy, where you move into accommodation closer to the training ground. You get to go to a new school – probably a better one than mine – and they sort out all your food and stuff."

He paused, letting her know that he was being serious. "I know I'm only eleven, but maybe you could ask if I could do that a year early … you know, just to help out."

Melanie looked at her son with a sad expression as she considered what he was saying.

Living on this estate and seeing the realities of life, such as sometimes struggling to afford enough food, had made Marcus more mature than a lot of boys his age.

But that didn't mean that he was ready to move out of their home. To her, he was still her little boy.

She was also wary of the world of football, especially after seeing how hard the academy worked their young players. She wasn't sure how well she could protect him from the more ruthless side of the business if she wasn't able to see him every day.

"I'd be less than an hour down the road," Marcus said, almost reading her mind. "Besides, I want to be a footballer, mum. I'm good at it. And that's the best way for me to do it."

Melanie smiled proudly, hearing Marcus's determination to achieve his dreams. She would do anything to support him in his ambition – and that included making sure he was getting the right food to eat. She had to admit that there was no guarantee he would get that here.

"OK," she said slowly, "I'll ring the club tomorrow. But if you're not happy there, Marcus Rashford, you're to come straight home – no matter how much you want to be a footballer."

5
CUTTING DAY

May 2009, Manchester United training ground, Manchester

Moving into the academy's accommodation had been tougher than Marcus had thought it would be.

His family were still close by, but not sleeping under the same roof as them had taken a long time to get used to, and he found himself missing the strangest of things – simple things, like his brothers pushing him around or his mum nagging him.

Luckily, being so close to home meant he was able to see them every weekend, and Dwaine often took him to the Trafford Centre Soccer Dome in central Manchester, to show him off in five-a-side matches against random teams.

For Marcus, those five-a-sides with Dwaine were a refreshing change from football at the academy, which was always so pressurised and so serious.

There were some days when Marcus felt homesick, missing being around his mum and his brothers, but on those days he would just remind himself that, by being at the academy, he was helping his mum out.

Then he would distract himself with the football. Academy football *was* serious, but it was also top quality, and Marcus could feel himself going from strength to strength, slowly inching closer to his dream of playing professionally.

Today's academy session was going very well. In fact, Marcus was sure he was having the best training session of his life. Every ball was killed with his first touch, every pass found the feet of a team-mate and every shot rippled the back of the net. He even managed to flip-flap an opponent successfully for the first time, flicking the ball between the outside and inside of his foot, before pinging it through his opponent's legs.

Such a good session couldn't have come at a better time for Marcus, because today was his first 'Cutting Day'.

That wasn't the official name for the day, but that's what all the older academy boys called it, and Marcus thought it was a pretty accurate name for it.

The Man United programme that Marcus had joined – a year early – was really competitive and, at the end of every season, players were cut from the academy squad, with only a select few allowed to progress to the next year.

And, with each year that passed, new boys from all over the country joined the academy, so the competition became even fiercer.

Marcus liked this way of doing things. He knew the pressure would make him up his game and help him get closer to his goal of being a professional footballer.

But as he met his mum after today's training session, he could see straight away how much she hated the pressure he was being put under.

"Whatever happens, you know I'll support you," she said quietly, as they took their seats in a waiting room with the other youth players and parents.

Marcus just smiled at her. Despite what others said, he was sure that Cutting Day was just a way to get rid of the boys who weren't taking training seriously – boys who spent their time messing around. He wished he could reassure his mum that really there was nothing to worry about.

After a few minutes Marcus saw his friend Matt emerging from the office across the waiting room, followed by the rest of his family.

"Who's that?" his mum whispered, following Marcus's gaze.

"That's Matt," Marcus replied, matching her tone. "He's definitely going to get through – he's one of the best players here. And he scored in the last game."

Marcus waited for Matt to get a little closer, then went over to say hello. As Marcus stood facing him, he realised that Matt had been crying.

Marcus suddenly felt his body go tense.

If Matt had been cut, then maybe Marcus had it all

wrong. Maybe they weren't just getting rid of the boys who messed about all the time. And that meant that Marcus wasn't safe either.

Then, as he heard some whispers at the back of the waiting room about Matt being 'too small', thoughts of all the good things Marcus had achieved this season suddenly evaporated.

All he could think about were the few times in training when he'd fired a penalty high and wide, missing the goal, or how there might be things wrong with him that he couldn't help – like his height.

Marcus felt his mum's hand holding his, giving it a reassuring squeeze, but thankfully his time for worrying was over.

"Marcus Rashford, would you like to come on in."

Marcus and his mum sat themselves down, facing the Head of Youth Development across his desk.

He greeted them warmly, then got straight on to business.

"How do you think the season's gone, Marcus?"

Marcus froze for a second, not quite sure what the right answer was. Should he act confident and cocky?

Or should he try and be a bit more modest?

"Yeah, I think it's been alright," he said, deciding to go down the middle, "I've had some good games and good moments, but I think I've still got a lot to do to improve."

The head nodded and leaned back in his chair. "I think we're all agreed here that you're actually one of the best players to come through the academy."

It took a moment for Marcus to make sense of what he was being told. David Beckham, Gary Neville, Danny Welbeck and Paul Pogba had all come through this academy – and now they were telling him that they considered him to be one of the best. That had to mean he wasn't being cut. Didn't it?

"Marcus?" the coach probed.

"Yes? Sorry, I was just taking it all in," Marcus babbled, looking at the two faces in the room – both of them smiling at him.

"I was just offering you the chance to stay with us for another year," the coach said again.

Relief surged through Marcus's body, and he found himself almost shouting his answer.

"Yes! I'd love to!"

6

CAPTAIN'S ORDERS

September 2015, De Herdgang, the Netherlands
Manchester United U19 v PSV Eindhoeven U19

Marcus proudly strapped the captain's armband around his arm. Today he was leading the U19s team in the UEFA Youth League, in an away game at PSV in the Netherlands, and he had one thing on his mind.

He wanted to use this opportunity get the attention of Man United's first team manager, Louis van Gaal.

As he tied up his bootlaces, Marcus thought about

all the changes he'd seen at the top, as he'd worked his way up through the academy, surviving Cutting Day year after year.

When he'd first arrived Sir Alex Ferguson had been in charge, but then the legendary manager had retired and had been replaced by David Moyes.

That had worried Marcus at the time. Moyes didn't have a reputation for bringing through young players from the academy, and Marcus had known that United were bound to spend millions to support the new manager.

That would mean that a string of world superstars would be getting into the first team – ahead of him.

But Marcus needn't have worried. Moyes had lasted just one year before being sacked, and he'd been replaced temporarily by Ryan Giggs, and then permanently by Louis van Gaal – a Dutch manager of world renown who, to Marcus's delight, had a reputation for blooding younger players.

Marcus was yet to make his debut for the first team, but today, as captain for the U19s, he was hopeful that playing well in this game would go some way towards changing that.

"Come on, boys," he called out, rallying his team, "let's treat this like it's the Champions League."

As soon as the whistle went he led by example, pressing the defenders whenever they looked vulnerable.

Marcus had struggled with a growth spurt a few years ago, which at the time had caused a worrying dip in his performance.

Luckily, the club had been patient with him while he'd learnt to work with his taller physique, and now pace was one of his main weapons. Combined with his natural awareness for the game, he knew how to use it sensibly and efficiently.

It wasn't long before they won a free kick and Marcus stood over the ball with Callum McGribbin.

"You want this one, Cap?" Callum asked.

Marcus looked at the goal and then back at the position of the ball. He wanted to get on the scoresheet, but he could see that the angle was more suited to a left-footed player.

"No, you take it," he replied. "I think it might suit you better."

Marcus was right. Callum stepped up and whipped the ball into the top right-hand corner.

Marcus's chance to join Callum on the scoresheet came a couple of minutes into the second half, when the ref pointed to the spot.

Marcus stepped up and slammed the penalty high and hard into the top right-hand corner. The keeper stood no chance and Marcus heard ripples of applause from the small crowd who were watching.

The game got back underway, and Marcus continued to be United's main threat.

When Tyler Reid got the ball out on the right-hand side, he knew exactly where it was going. He drifted into the space in between PSV's two centre-backs, meaning that neither of them knew exactly where he was.

He then played an inch-perfect ball over to Marcus, who flicked it into the far corner, sealing United's 3-0 win.

Arms out like an airplane, Marcus wheeled away to the corner flag, hoping that Louis van Gaal was watching.

7

BRACE YOURSELVES

February 2016, Old Trafford, Manchester, England
Manchester United v Midtjylland

Marcus's head had been spinning all day.

Man United were in the middle of an injury crisis and, with the January transfer window now closed, they were seriously short of options when it came to strikers.

As a result, Marcus had been called up to be on the bench for today's game – a home tie in the Europa League against Danish club FC Midtjylland.

As Marcus joined in the pre-game warm-up, he looked excitedly around the Old Trafford ground, praying that he'd get 10 minutes at the end of the match.

That certainly wasn't guaranteed. Marcus wasn't even playing regularly for the reserves yet, so the manager would probably try at all costs to avoid putting him on.

That's what had happened on the only other occasion he'd been called up to the bench as a result of this injury crisis.

Still, just to be on the bench proved to Marcus that his efforts to get himself on Louis van Gaal's radar were working, and he relished this opportunity. Just being a part of a match-day was a great experience.

Marcus had started running on the spot, picking up his knees to keep himself loose, when out of the corner of his eye he suddenly glimpsed a red shirt moving slowly.

It was Anthony Martial, and he was hobbling off the pitch, with the help of the club's medical team.

Marcus just stood there watching him, trying to process what that might mean.

Anthony was supposed to be in the starting eleven today – and he was a striker. And now he was injured ...

Marcus tried to contain his excitement, in case things weren't what they seemed. Perhaps the Frenchman was playing a joke on somebody, or perhaps this was some kind of drill the first team did, to see how fast physios could respond. Or perhaps ...

Then Marcus heard a voice bellowing his name across the pitch. The shout came from Louis van Gaal.

Marcus instantly jogged over to the manager, trying to ignore the little flips in his stomach.

"Anthony's out," Louis said. "So you're going to be our striker for today. Can you do that?"

Marcus was nodding before his brain had even caught up with the situation. He was going to make his Manchester United debut. And it wasn't going to be five or 10 minutes at the end of the match – he was going to be starting as a striker.

Finally he was living the dream he'd decided on in this very stadium as a five-year-old boy.

As Louis marched off to alert his coaching assistants to the last-minute change, Marcus started scanning the stands, trying to find Dwaine. He knew he was up there somewhere, and he wondered if he'd be able to let his brother know in some way.

Marcus quickly gave up – all he could see was a sea of faces. But it didn't matter as Dwaine would soon find out.

After following his team-mates back into the dressing room, it wasn't long before Marcus found himself walking back out on to the pitch, feeling as if he was ten feet tall.

He knew that he was good enough to take this opportunity with both hands – he just had to stay calm and focused.

But, with all the adrenaline coursing through his body, he started the game at a frenetic pace.

"Marcus!"

He turned to find Ander Herrera, United's midfield general, looking at him.

"Calm down," Herrera went on, "don't waste all your energy in the first five minutes or you'll blow up. Save yourself."

Marcus nodded, not entirely sure how Herrera even

knew his name, and did his best to follow the Spaniard's advice.

He desperately wanted to give United the opening goal, but Pione Sisto gave it to the opposition instead, firing Midtjylland ahead after 28 minutes.

Luckily, Memphis Depay brought United back level, skipping away down the left-hand side and firing a cross into the box, where it was diverted into the back of the net by a Midtjylland defender.

Marcus had just started to punch the air in celebration when he noticed that the rest of the team were already rushing back to the half-way line to restart the game.

He'd almost forgotten that this was the second leg of a knockout match, and that United were still 3-2 down on aggregate.

Come half-time United were still trailing on aggregate, and Marcus sat on his own in a corner of the dressing room.

Sensing his anxiety, Michael Carrick, captain for the evening, walked over to talk to him.

"You're doing good out there, kid," Carrick said,

sitting down next to him. "Don't worry, the goal's going to come for you. I'm sure of it."

Marcus didn't think he could express how much that vote of confidence meant to him, so he just gave his captain a little nod and decided he would thank him by playing the best football of his life in the second half – the kind of football that would earn him a permanent place in this squad.

Fifteen minutes into the second half, a Guillermo Varela cross came to Juan Mata at the back post. Mata controlled it, then fired it back into the middle of the box.

Marcus had seen it coming, and in that moment everything went silent, as if he was underwater. He held his breath and moved in to crash the ball towards the net …

Watching the ball cross the line, Marcus suddenly felt as if he'd come up for air, as the deafening noise in the stadium hit him.

GOAL!

Marcus was sprinting past his overjoyed team-mates, not completely sure where he was going, when he spotted a group of teenage fans behind the barriers. This morning he'd been one of them, looking forward excitedly to watching this game – but now he was the Manchester United goalscorer!

He ploughed into the fans and felt them hugging him, clapping him on the back and rubbing his head.

Then his team-mates caught up with him and dragged him back on to the pitch.

"Great goal, kid, but we haven't won yet," someone roared over the sound of the crowd. "We need another one!"

Twelve minutes later, Marcus's good evening turned into a great one. Varela whipped a cross into the box where he was waiting and he met the ball with his right foot, steering it into the bottom corner.

GOAL!

Marcus sprinted back towards the same set of fans, slapping the corner flag as he passed it. He was in a state of total euphoria.

He'd scored a brace on his debut!

Late goals from Ander Herrera and Memphis Depay meant that United ultimately ran out 5-1 winners, and at full time Marcus was so elated he could barely speak.

Instead, he just stood on the pitch, looking around the magnificent stadium, soaking up the atmosphere so that he could remember this moment for the rest of his life.

8
ONLY DOUBLES

February 2016, Old Trafford, Manchester
Manchester United v Arsenal

Marcus pulled his socks up nervously. It had only been three days since the Europa League match, but his two goals had catapulted him into the national spotlight and the days had been crazy.

Thinking about those two goals still gave him goosebumps. His mum had cried with happiness when he'd seen her afterwards, and Dwaine had been ecstatic for him. Even Dave Horrocks had been on the phone, saying he was going to add him to the Fletcher Moss Rangers wall of fame, right next to Wes Brown.

But now the pressure was on – the world of football wanted to know if Marcus could do it again. And could he do it against a Premier League title-chasing side?

They were about to find out.

United were taking on Arsenal at home and, with Anthony Martial, Will Keane and Wayne Rooney all still out, Marcus was once again in the squad.

As he lined up in the tunnel, he realised that he was a lot more nervous than last time.

For one, he'd known in advance that he'd be playing today, so he'd had time to think about it and feel the pressure build up.

Two, this was his Premier League debut, and that definitely meant more to him.

And three, he was well aware that people were expecting something from him today, especially as this tie was historically one of the biggest games in English football – and one that United had dominated in recent memory.

Marcus took a deep breath and pushed all those thoughts to the back of his mind. This was just another game, and he was going to give it his all.

Out on the pitch, he took a second to take in the Arsenal team, which included quality players like Mesut Özil and Alexis Sánchez.

It was a strong side, and for the first 20 minutes Arsenal pinned United in their own half, dominating the ball.

But in the 29th minute things changed. Varela fired in a fierce cross that Arsenal could only half-clear, and the ball flicked towards Marcus.

He met it with his right foot, slamming it towards the goal.

Petr Čech got a glove to it, but the shot was too strong and the ball whistled into the top corner.

GOAL!

Now Marcus had his first goal in the Premier League!

He ran towards the corner of the pitch, leaping high into the air and punching the sky as his team-mates ran after him.

And then, a few moments later, the dream week

continued. Jesse Lingard got the ball and lifted it into the centre of the box, where Marcus was waiting.

Rising high above the defenders around him, Marcus met the ball with his head and sent it bouncing along the ground, beyond the desperate reach of Čech.

GOAL!

For the fourth time in his two games, Marcus felt his team-mates huddled around him. He could only look up at the sky and hope that the chances to play and win with every one of his team-mates would never end.

At full time, when United had run out 3-2 winners, Marcus felt as if he was floating around the pitch.

Then he came face-to-face with Danny Welbeck.

"I hear you're another Fletcher Moss Rangers and United Academy boy."

Marcus nodded, not sure in his excitement that he'd be able to speak full sentences.

"Well, you were brilliant out there. Dave will be raving at the TV," Welbeck said, as he started to walk away.

Marcus grinned, then continued to walk around shaking the hands of the other Arsenal players.

The players he'd just defeated.

9
VAN GAAL'S BEST

March 2016, Manchester United training ground, Manchester

"You're trying too hard."

Eyes wide, Marcus looked up into his manager's face.

Apart from that one occasion when he'd been told that he was going on against Midtjylland, Marcus hadn't had a one-on-one conversation with Louis van Gaal – and it was a bit intimidating now to have him standing in front of him in the middle of this training session.

Marcus had stopped training with the reserves and was now only training with the first team. He hoped that this wasn't the manager's way of telling him that this was over.

"You're quick, but you take too many touches with the ball," Louis went on in a thick Dutch accent.

"OK," Marcus said nervously.

"I want you to shoot early, and shoot hard," Louis went on. "Catch the keeper off guard."

Marcus knew Louis's criticisms were probably right. He often liked to try a trick or two, something he'd picked up from watching the two Ronaldos (Brazilian and Portuguese) on YouTube, but he knew that when they did that they were really just showboating.

The vast majority of their goals were tap-ins and hard shots – which meant being in the right place at the right time.

He thought back to that goal of Ronaldo's he'd seen at Old Trafford when he was younger, and what Dwaine had said.

"*Did you see how early he took that shot? Barthez didn't have a chance to set himself.*"

"I can do that, boss," he replied.

"Good lad." Louis paused. "You're doing well, Marcus. I know this must all be a bit of a shock for you."

Marcus smiled at the praise. It meant more hearing this from his manager than from anybody else in the world – but he felt a small pang of sadness as well.

Such spectacular debuts had changed his life practically overnight, and it had all turned out to be more than 'a bit of a shock'.

He recalled going to play a game of five-a-side at the Trafford Centre Soccer Dome, with Dwaine and some of their mates, about a week after the Arsenal match.

He'd expected it to be just a kick-about, just as it always used to be, but a couple of people had recognised him and that 'couple of people' had quickly turned into a crowd.

In the end he and Dwaine had had no choice but to leave.

It was sad thinking he'd never really get to play there again. That had been his little bolt-hole while he was growing up at the academy, a special place for him – and now it couldn't be that for him any more.

Still, that was a sacrifice, along with many others, that Marcus was willing to make to achieve his goal, and he wanted his new manager to know that.

"I can handle it," he said to Louis. "Anything is worth being a part of the first team. This is my dream."

Louis's lips curled into a smile. "Do you know how many young players I've brought through, Marcus?"

Marcus shook his head.

"I don't know either," Louis replied, "but I can tell you some of their names. Xavi, Andrés Iniesta, Patrick Kluivert, Clarence Seedorf, Carles Puyol, Thomas Müller, David Alaba … "

He paused and looked at Marcus straight in the eye.

"Forget the first team, son. Work with me and I'll make you into one of the best in the world."

10

THE DERBY DEBUT

March 2016, Etihad Stadium, Manchester
Manchester United v Manchester City

"First derby?" Jesse Lingard asked Marcus, as they walked from the dressing room to the Etihad tunnel.

Since starting training with the first squad, Marcus had formed a close relationship with Jesse. He was a fellow academy graduate and another local lad – he was fun, too, and reminded Marcus of his brothers.

"Yeah," Marcus replied. "Any advice?"

"Well, to be honest with you, Rash," Jesse grinned, "this is only my second one, so I know about as much as you do!"

Marcus shook his head. Jesse seemed to have such boundless confidence, he often forgot that this was Jesse's first proper season playing in the United first team as well, as he'd spent most of his time on loan at clubs in the Championship.

"Just remember it's your derby debut," Jesse went on. "And we all know what you do on your debuts!"

Marcus smiled and then took his place in the line, getting back to preparing mentally for the game.

Louis had been true to his word and had stuck with Marcus up front for the last few games, despite the fact that Anthony Martial was back in the squad. Marcus hadn't scored any more goals since his first two games, but he was determined to get one today.

Today's game was particularly important. It was important for the club, as they were competing with City for a place in the top four, but Marcus knew first-hand what this local derby meant to the fans.

This match was about whether the fans could go to

school – or to work – tomorrow with their heads held high, and he didn't want to let the United supporters down.

And even though City had won the league in two of the previous four seasons, they weren't untouchable. His manager had even identified ageing centre-back Martín Demichelis as a particularly weak link.

Marcus thought back to Louis's words in the dressing room earlier in the day.

"Demichelis is our target. For all his strengths, he doesn't have any pace and he's not agile. If you run at him and get him twisting and turning, you'll get an opportunity – you just have to make sure you finish it."

Suddenly Marcus felt Chris Smalling's hands on his back pushing him forward – they were walking out on to the pitch.

The atmosphere inside the Etihad was equal to that of Old Trafford, but Marcus knew instantly that he wasn't at home here – that he wasn't welcome.

The rest of the United players no doubt felt the same hostility, and for the first 15 minutes City's experienced team, that included the likes of Yaya Touré, Sergio

Agüero and David Silva, were utterly dominant – until Juan Mata managed to fire the ball into Marcus's path.

Marcus suddenly found himself one-on-one with their target, Demichelis, a man with half a century of caps for Argentina. The centre-back stretched to win the ball and Marcus saw an opportunity. He flicked the ball between his legs and ran around him.

A moment later he was in the box. Joe Hart made himself big in the goal, but Marcus spotted a gap, opened up his body and passed the ball into the bottom corner.

GOAL!

He'd scored the opening goal in the Manchester derby!

Marcus sprinted towards the corner, as was becoming his habit, ready to celebrate with the fans, but he looked up and saw a sea of miserable faces in light-blue shirts. He quickly turned back towards his team-mates and was embraced by Anthony Martial.

"Don't celebrate in front of *them*, man!" Jesse laughed, racing over to join them.

Jesse pulled Marcus in for a hug as soon as Anthony

had released him. "What is it with you and debuts, Rash?"

The rest of the game was all City. United were on the back foot and Marcus was barely involved in the game, with chances and touches being few and far between.

When the match eventually ended, despite City's dominance, the score was still 1-0 and Marcus had the incredible sensation of walking off the pitch knowing that he'd scored the winner.

He was halfway down the tunnel when he felt Jesse's weight on his back again.

"Mata's back there saying you'll never top that," Jesse shouted. "I reckon he's right. You're the youngest Manchester derby goalscorer in Premier League history! You've peaked already!"

Marcus laughed, but he couldn't agree.

He *would* top that. He was actually starting to feel unstoppable every time he pulled on his United shirt.

II
FA CUP FALL

May 2016, Wembley Stadium, London
Manchester United v Crystal Palace

Marcus could only imagine how it would feel to score a goal that won a trophy.

That, he thought, would be the perfect way to end this whirlwind season, a season he'd started by playing in the Youth Cup and ended by playing in the big leagues.

But today he had the chance to do exactly that,

because today was FA Cup Final day – Man United were playing Crystal Palace.

But for Marcus a goal just didn't seem to be coming.

The game was slow and hard-fought, and although Marcus was trying to be as creative as possible, to use his vision to find a way to unlock the opposition's defence, he just couldn't make it happen.

Then, halfway through the second half, he found himself on the floor after a tussle with Zaha. Cabaye followed in, landing on Marcus's knee, and Marcus cried out in pain.

He was sure it was only an impact injury, but he knew that he couldn't stay on the pitch. Clearly, Louis was of the same opinion and Marcus saw his number go up.

After so many dream debuts and important goals, limping off the pitch with an FA Cup final at 0-0 made Marcus feel that he'd failed.

But as the physio looked him over, Marcus decided to take this moment to reflect on things.

He'd had a great season, and he had played well today, but he wasn't quite 'there' yet. He still had a lot of work to do before he would become the kind of player who changed big games like today's, but he knew that Louis was onboard with getting him to that stage.

He did, however, still want to lift his first professional trophy.

It didn't look as if that was going to happen today, as he sat on the bench and watched Palace take the lead.

But then Juan Mata equalised, taking the game to extra time.

Marcus watched with bated breath as a Delaney block suddenly fell to the feet of Jesse, just inside the area. Marcus raised his hands to his face as he watched his friend thunder in a volley which left Hennessey stranded.

GOAL!

Marcus wished he was celebrating the goal with his team-mates on the pitch, but all the same he hugged the other lads on the bench and watched excitedly as United held out for a 2-1 win.

When the final whistle went, half the stadium erupted.

At one moment Marcus was running back on to the

pitch, celebrating with the players, and then he was climbing the famous Wembley steps and jumping around with his team as Wayne Rooney held the beautiful cup aloft.

Marcus brushed the silver confetti off his face and took a moment to look out over the stadium, lingering on the Wembley steps while the others returned to the pitch to parade the trophy around.

"Playing here for England is even more nuts than this," Wayne Rooney said, standing next to Marcus and looking at the same scene.

Marcus suddenly noticed that Rooney had held back to wait for him, and he smiled. It only felt like yesterday that he and a group of friends at the academy were camping out outside the canteen, hoping to run into the United legend, and now Marcus could call him a mate.

Yet he knew what Wayne was referring to. There were rumours that Marcus might be getting a spot in the Euros 2016 preliminary squad – but Marcus didn't want to think about that now. It was just too surreal.

"I think I still prefer Old Trafford," Marcus said with a wink, turning to go and have his turn with the trophy.

12
THE THREE LIONS

May 2016, Stadium of Light, Sunderland
England v Australia

As Marcus pulled his England shirt over his head, he had to fight the urge to pinch himself.

The rumours had been true – and the call-up from Roy Hodgson, the current England manager, had indeed come.

"After your performance this season, I think there would be riots in the streets if I didn't have you in my

England squad," Roy had told Marcus over the phone.

And now Marcus was standing in the only shirt (other than his Man United one) that he'd ever been interested in wearing, about to make his international debut in a friendly against Australia.

"That suits you, Rash," Wayne said, sitting next to him in the dressing room.

Marcus turned and grinned at Rooney, pleased to have Wayne's familiar face near him. Being surrounded by strikers such as Kane, Vardy and Sterling was a little overwhelming, even though they'd all been very supportive.

After the reality check of the FA Cup Final match, Marcus had to be sure he was playing his very best game from the moment the whistle went – and within three minutes the dream goal happened.

Sterling's deflected cross had whipped up into the air, and Marcus kept his eyes on the ball as it came his way, coming towards it and meeting it with his right foot.

It wasn't his best volley, and he didn't catch it cleanly. But he had time to turn and watch as the ball skimmed off the ground and past the Australian keeper.

GOAL!

He'd done it again!

As his team-mates started to mob him, Marcus couldn't work out who was saying what over the din of the crowd – a crowd that was now going wild, celebrating their nation's latest hero.

"You make debuts look easy!"

"You won't forget that one, kid!"

After the excitement of scoring, for Marcus the rest of the game was a blur and he almost had to double-check the score as he came off the pitch.

A member of the coaching staff chuckled at him and confirmed England had won 2-1.

"Oh, and Marcus," the coach continued, "you should know you're now the youngest England player to score on his debut for almost 80 years."

13

WHO WANTS TO WIN THE PREMIER LEAGUE?

July 2016, Manchester United training ground, Manchester

Marcus knew that football was a ruthless business – the Cutting Days at the academy had taught him that – but he often forgot that it was exactly the same for managers.

They had their 'cutting days' too.

A reminder had come within 24 hours of Man United's FA Cup win. United hadn't done enough to secure a spot in the top four in the league, and the FA Cup on its own wasn't enough to save Louis.

So now Marcus was sitting with the rest of the squad, waiting to meet their latest manager.

Feeling on edge, Marcus started jiggling his foot. He'd known that he'd been in favour with Louis, that the manager had believed in him – after all, Louis had told him that.

But Marcus didn't have that security with this new manager, who was a very divisive character. He was also known for not playing younger players.

The thought made Marcus jiggle his foot a little more vigorously.

The fact that his confidence had taken a knock over the summer wasn't helping his nerves. His fantastic England debut had earned him a spot in the 2016 Euros squad, but it hadn't gone well.

England had been knocked out of the tournament by minnows Iceland. Marcus had only played in two of the games, so he was spared a lot of the criticism, but it wasn't how he'd imagined his first international tournament would go.

The players all looked up at the door, hearing footsteps approaching. Marcus stopped jiggling his foot, planting it firmly on the floor, as the players watched the door swung open to reveal José Mourinho.

The new United manager walked straight into the middle of the room and then started eyeing up each of the players in turn.

"Who wants to win the Premier League?" he asked after a long silence, his voice echoing around the hushed room.

Some of the players nodded and a couple nervously raised their hands.

"You stick with me, you support me, and I'll get you there," José continued. "I'll put silverware in your hands. Everywhere I've been, I've won. So trust me, I know how to win titles."

He paused, as if he was daring anyone to disagree with him, though a quick glance around the room showed Marcus that his team-mates, like him, were hanging off José's every word.

"Now, nobody here is above the team, and nobody here is below the team. You show me that you can work hard and that you can do what I ask of you, and you'll be in my team. If not, I am more than happy to show you where the door is."

José gestured at the door he'd just walked through.

"There will be some new signings coming to the club. But if you show me what you can do, show me how you can play, then they won't be *replacements*. They will be colleagues."

And with that, Mourinho disappeared into his office, calling in the players one at a time to speak with them individually.

As Marcus waited for his turn to go in, he tapped out a quick text message to Dwaine.

> He's terrifying. And he's bringing in new signings like I thought. I just don't think he's going to play me.

Dwaine had been waiting for Marcus's text, eager to hear what the infamous manager was really like in person. He replied to his brother in seconds.

> Cool! Work hard and he'll play you. Remember what he did to Eden Hazard? He basically played him as a left-back, so just be up for whatever he wants.

Marcus wished he shared Dwaine's enthusiasm, although at the very least he could see his brother's point about Hazard. And he didn't mind taking on defensive work, such as tracking back.

He felt his phone vibrate again and read a second message from his brother.

> Wherever Jose is trophies always follow. This is a good thing bro!

Suddenly, Marcus heard a coaching assistant calling his name. Shoving his phone into his pocket, he nervously made his way into Mourinho's office.

"Marcus!" José said with a warm smile, gesturing for him to take a seat opposite him.

José wasn't particularly imposing as a man, but he carried himself with the aura of someone who'd won two Champions Leagues, three Premier Leagues and whole lot more on top. Marcus could feel himself being inspired by Mourinho's confidence.

"So, Marcus, tell me, what are your plans for this season?" José asked. "What do you want to achieve?"

"Well, I mean, I want to play as many games as possible," Marcus said.

He'd expected this meeting to be mainly José talking at him, and he was a little caught off guard by the question.

"And, uh, I want to score as many goals as possible – maybe 20? And win trophies, too."

"OK, and where do you see yourself playing?"

"I'm happy to play anywhere," he said quickly, thinking about Dwaine's text.

"That's good to hear," José replied, nodding his head. Then he leaned forward. "I want you to know that I see you as an important part of my squad, Marcus. We're giving you the number 19 shirt to show that. But you should know that I'm going to be bringing in Zlatan Ibrahimovic as our main striker … "

Marcus hoped that José hadn't noticed his reaction to his manager's mention of the striker's name.

He'd been expecting some big signings, but Zlatan Ibrahimovic was on another level. The legendary striker had scored goals all over Europe. Marcus simply couldn't compete with that – at least, not after the one good half season he'd just had.

"… so you might find yourself playing from the left wing more often than not," José continued. "I don't want that to worry you – many players can influence the game from the left wing."

"Will that require more defensive work?" Marcus asked. "I'm happy to do it, by the way," he added.

José nodded, and Marcus could tell that he was sizing him up.

"It might require a little bit more, yes. But it's important for the team. And, if you want to win, I'm sure you won't even notice that you're doing the extra work."

14
JOSÉ AT THE WHEEL

October 2016, Stamford Bridge, London
Manchester United v Chelsea

Marcus trudged into the dressing room with the rest of the United team, letting their 4-0 defeat against Chelsea sink in. He collapsed on to his seat and looked around, watching everyone else's reactions.

Ibra's face depicted a terrifying mix of calm and anger. Marcus hadn't yet spoken to the Swede, and he certainly wouldn't be choosing this moment to do that.

Paul Pogba, who'd also been a big-money arrival, looked disappointed, but not particularly nervous. But then again, thought Marcus, after costing the club £90 million he was hardly going to be dropped.

Marcus had no such security – and he was beginning to feel the pressure. Following his dream first season, now it just felt as if everything was going wrong.

He'd gone from a manager, Louis van Gaal – who was planning to turn him into one of the greats – to a manager who he wasn't even sure was going to play him from one game to the next.

Indeed, after earning a medal for playing 20 minutes in the Community Shield, Marcus had become more of an occasional player under José Mourinho, and he'd only scored four goals so far this season – the same number of goals he'd bagged in just his first two games last season.

And today he'd been handed a rare start – a whole 90 minutes – and he'd wasted it. Instead of showing José what he could do, he'd just shown him what he *couldn't* do – that he struggled to cope with the defensive duties of tracking Chelsea's wing-back, Victor Moses.

When Mourinho finally stormed into the dressing room he was in a foul mood, having argued with opposite manager Antonio Conte about the Chelsea celebrations – and Marcus was horrified to hear José calling him out by name.

"Marcus!" José bellowed, "you have to work hard in my team, you have to track back, you have to defend! Were you doing that today?"

Marcus didn't know where to look, embarrassed that he was being singled out.

"But he still ran twice as far as any of you lot ran!" José continued, turning on the rest of the team.

The squad sat in silence as he continued his tirade.

"Look, lads. I don't want to be critical, I don't want to be hurtful," he said, now speaking quietly, "but I know you can play much better than this."

Marcus looked at the floor, wondering for the first time in his career if that was even true.

Maybe, as Jesse had joked after his derby debut, he'd already peaked.

15
THE DROUGHT

December 2016, Marcus's mum's house, Manchester

Lying on the sofa, playing FIFA with Dwaine, Marcus felt like himself, the *real* Marcus, for the first time in a long time.

He certainly needed a break from being José's 'Number 19, Rashford'.

United weren't doing well. They were in sixth place, nine points off Man City who were in fourth place and a massive 13 points adrift of Chelsea, who were leading the pack. People were starting to talk.

But, even worse than that, Marcus was in the middle of a goal drought, having failed to score in any competition since September.

This was incredibly concerning for a young attacking player, and whenever talk of it cropped up in the media, along with rumours that he was going to be loaned out, he had to leave the room.

He just couldn't face hearing about it.

It was already keeping him up at night. He would lie in bed for hours, staring up at his white ceiling and seeing the criss-cross of goal netting ingrained on it.

But more than anything, Marcus just missed the rush of scoring. Bringing fans to their feet was all he'd ever wanted to do, and it was frustrating to be stuck in this vicious cycle of getting only 10 or 20 minutes out on the wing because he wasn't scoring or playing well, and not scoring or playing well because he was only getting 10 or 20 minutes out on the wing.

It just wasn't enough time in the right position to make an impact.

And now, playing FIFA against his brother, he was still struggling to make an impact. He watched as Dwaine weaved his way through his United defence to score the winner.

"God, there's no fight in you today. That's the third time I've wiped the floor with you!" Dwaine said, throwing a cushion at him.

Marcus sighed, pushed the cushion aside and rested his controller on top of it.

"Sorry," he said, starting to massage his temples. "I just can't shake this feeling that my United career is over before it's even begun. I'm literally spending all my time just waiting for the call that says they're going to drop me or sell me."

"Stop being a baby," his brother replied straight away.

Marcus looked around, a little surprised – he'd expected *some* sympathy, or at the very least the chance to talk about it.

"You're nineteen years old," Dwaine went on, "playing Premier League football for your dream club, under the best manager in the world, with some of the best players in the world."

Marcus already knew what his brother was saying, but even so he needed to hear it out loud. He was already well aware that it was Dwaine who'd been keeping his feet on the ground, ever since his first day at the academy.

"Whatever you need to do, put the work in," Dwaine continued. "If he wants you to be fitter, spend a bit longer in the gym. If you want to play as a striker, ask for the chance to prove yourself. If you need to improve, learn from the people around you."

As Dwaine spoke, Marcus could feel a new sense of purpose. His brother was right. Marcus had every reason to want to pull himself out of this slump, and he had every resource to help him do it.

"Seriously, bro. Regrow that backbone of yours." Dwaine looked over at Marcus with his eyebrows raised.

Marcus chuckled. He *did* have a backbone – and a good one at that. It had got him through the academy, through all those high-pressure debuts – and it could certainly get him through a goal drought and whatever came with playing under José Mourinho.

Turning back to the TV, Marcus picked up his controller and selected the option to 'Play again' on FIFA.

16

MARCUS'S BACKBONE

January 2017, Manchester United training ground,
Manchester

Marcus knocked firmly on José's office door, then pushed it open.

"Hi boss," he said, poking his head around the door, "can I have a quick word with you?"

"Alright, Marcus," José said, gesturing for him to come in and take a seat. "What's this about?"

"It's about the Reading game," Marcus replied,

referring to United's next game against Reading in the FA Cup. "I want to play up front – I want to play as a striker."

"I see," José replied, mulling it over. "To be honest with you Marcus, there were a few of us here who were thinking a loan move might be good for you. That would give you the opportunity to play up front regularly. Does that interest you at all?"

For a second, Marcus felt his stomach drop. The rumours he'd been hearing were true.

But he ignored the feeling, deciding instead to focus on the fire in his belly. He didn't want to be loaned out, sent away from the city that had been his home for his entire life.

Besides, Man United was the only club he'd ever been interested in playing for. His mum had worked hard to give him his chance here and he'd left home and moved to the academy to secure his chance with the club.

He hadn't gone through all that to see it come to nothing.

"To be honest, boss," he said finally, "I'd rather stay here. I've been at United since I was seven years old and

I don't want to leave. I want to stay and fight for my place in the side."

As he finished speaking, Marcus looked at his manager. He was sure he could see a new-found respect in his eyes.

"Very good then," José suddenly said, breaking into a smile. "You'll start up front against Reading. Don't let me down."

Out on the pitch at the start of the Reading game, Marcus felt a few nerves. He jumped up and down, trying to shake them out of his system.

"You'll do fine, Rash," Rooney said, behind him. "I've got your back."

Marcus gave Rooney a determined nod, but it was the Liverpudlian who got the first goal of the game, deflecting the ball in after Mata's pass.

And then it was Anthony Martial who added a second, coolly slotting the ball into the far corner.

Marcus had a chance of his own shortly after. He found himself skipping past the goalkeeper with the ball, but the movement took him wide and the angle was too tight. He couldn't wrap his foot round the ball – and it slammed into the side netting.

"Come on!" Marcus shouted, kicking the air in annoyance.

"Keep trying," Mata said, trying to calm him down. "It's going to come."

But Marcus didn't need reassuring. This goal drought was going to end today.

Marcus had a few more chances, each of them saved, but he kept on going, not allowing himself to look at Mourihno, who was standing on the touchline.

His next chance came when Michael Carrick's through-ball evaded the Reading defenders and landed at his feet.

He sprinted forward, brushing off the challenge of a second defender, and waited for the keeper to come out …

Then, seeing his chance, he coolly passed the ball into the far corner.

GOAL!

In the very moment that the ball crossed the line

Marcus felt as if the entire weight of Old Trafford had been lifted from his shoulders. He kept his celebration cool, jogging back to the half-way line and limiting the display of his utter elation to a small smile. But he did glance over at the touchline – to see José clapping.

And then, not long afterwards, as if he was proving a point, Marcus got his second.

He closed down the keeper as he always did, trying to put pressure on him, when the keeper miskicked the ball, which trickled towards the goal.

Marcus and the keeper both chased after it, but Marcus was quicker and he got there first, slamming it hard into the goal to seal the win for United.

Marcus was back – and whether he was moved back to the wing, given 10 minutes on the pitch, or given a dressing down by José – he wasn't going to let it stop him taking his football to the next level.

17
BECOME MORE LIKE ZLATAN

February 2017, Manchester United training ground,
Manchester

With the pressure of his goal drought lifted, Marcus quickly realised that his play on the pitch was improving considerably.

The goals still weren't coming as freely as he'd have liked, but he knew that he was having more of an impact on games.

His new sense of purpose remained with him, so after

today's training session he decided to work on one skill he'd always wanted to master: free kicks.

Or, more specifically, free kicks using Cristiano Ronaldo's knuckleball technique.

Marcus stood in front of an empty goal armed with five balls and started firing them towards it. He hit each ball in a way that minimised the spin, so that it would snake unpredictably through the air.

Then he'd retrieve the five balls and start again. He was on his third round when he sensed somebody standing behind him.

He turned and found himself face to face with Zlatan Ibrahimovic

"So, you want to be like Ronaldo, huh?" Ibra said, looking Marcus up and down disapprovingly.

Marcus had barely said ten words to the Swede since his arrival at the start of the season – he really was one of the most intimidating people Marcus had ever met.

Even now, standing there, part of him wanted to make an excuse and just run away. But then he thought about his conversation with Dwaine at Christmas.

He wanted to improve, and here he was, talking to

one of the best strikers of all time. Rather than continuing to moan about having to compete with him, Marcus needed to see this as an opportunity to learn from him.

He thought about Zlatan's question and answered it honestly.

"Well, I want to take free kicks like him."

"Why?" Ibra asked, bluntly.

"He scores them well. And I want to add more to my game," Marcus said. "Didn't you have any heroes you wanted to be like?"

"No," Ibra scoffed. "My only hero was Zlatan."

Marcus nodded, not quite sure what to say to that.

"I can help you, if you want," Ibra continued. "You can become more like Zlatan."

"Sure," Marcus said, breaking into a smile, thrilled that Ibra was offering the help that Marcus wanted, without his even asking for it.

"First of all," Ibra continued, "never try to be anyone else. Be your own man on the pitch."

"Not even you?" Marcus asked jokingly.

"Never ever try and be Zlatan," Ibra replied, looking

deadly serious. "That is a pinnacle no one will ever reach."

Then a small smile lit up his face. "Free kicks are a waste of time anyway. How many times do you get a free kick in this kind of position in a game?"

Marcus thought about it, and he knew the superstar had a point.

"Just practise your shooting," Ibra said, "and if you're going to watch clips of other people, forget the strikers. Instead, watch the goalkeepers you're up against. Some defend near-post, some defend the far post, but none of them can defend both. That's how you know what corner to aim for."

And with that, Ibra strolled back towards the changing rooms, leaving Marcus standing alone on the pitch, grateful that the guy was on *his* team.

Marcus was even more grateful that Ibra was on his team when the next game rolled around – a League Cup final against Southampton.

It was an opportunity for Man United to get their first

major trophy of the season and, even though Marcus was starting on the bench, he didn't let that deter him.

He stayed focused and watched as Ibra fired United into the lead with a whipped free kick, before Jesse doubled their lead 20 minutes later.

Following their chat after training, Marcus now felt a little more comfortable talking to Ibra, and at half-time he couldn't resist pointing out the irony of his goal.

"I thought you told me free kicks were a waste of time!" Marcus laughed.

"For you they are," Ibra replied. "Not for Zlatan."

The second half was more frustrating to watch, as United threw away their two-goal lead, allowing Southampton back into the game.

It wasn't until the 77th minute that Marcus was summoned on, to replace Jesse.

As he walked on to the pitch, high-fiving his friend, he remembered his thoughts last year at the FA Cup final. He desperately wanted to get the goal that secured a trophy.

Unfortunately, today wasn't the day, and instead it

was Zlatan who headed home the winner for Man United.

Together with the rest of the team, Marcus ran over to Ibra to celebrate the victory with him.

"You have to give me more lessons, how to become more like Zlatan! I need to know how to do that!" Marcus bellowed.

Ibra just winked at him, then turned back to the crowd with his arms out wide, as if he was going to take a bow.

Minutes later, Marcus had a medal around his neck and was celebrating the second major trophy of his career.

Looking out at the euphoric faces in the stands, he was already planning the impact he was going to make when they played for the next one.

18
LIVERPOOL'S PERCH

March 2018, Old Trafford Stadium, Manchester
Manchester United v Liverpool

As the season played out Marcus didn't just become more like Zlatan – he actively filled in for him, taking his place on the pitch.

The Swede had been injured in a quarter-final Europa League tie against Anderlecht, a game in which Marcus had gone on to score the winner.

Marcus had scored in the semi-final, and then he'd

led the line in the final against Ajax, which Man United had won.

Marcus was annoyed that he hadn't scored in the final, but he was proud to add a third trophy to his collection and to qualify his team for Champions League football next year – even though they'd only finished in sixth place in the League.

The European success naturally meant that José had been given money to buy additional players, and it was another busy summer, with Victor Lindelöf, Nemanja Matic and Romelu Lukaku all arriving for huge fees.

But this time Marcus wasn't disheartened. Even though Rom was a striker, which meant that Marcus was finding himself out on the wing again, he knew he just needed to keep putting the work in.

And today was no exception – because today they were taking on Liverpool.

It was a huge match, as a win would mean that Man United were still in with an outside chance of catching Man City for the title – and, more important, they would move several points clear of Liverpool, their fiercest rivals.

As he walked on to the pitch, Marcus thought about the times when these two clubs had met when he was a child.

Each time it had felt as if it was a matter of life or death. After all, Ferguson had once said that his sole aim while leading United was to 'knock Liverpool off their perch', as they'd been dominating English football for so long.

And, for as long as Marcus could remember, United had done just that. Liverpool hadn't won a title for a long time – although in recent years they had started looking dangerous again.

Today he needed to play in a way that his younger self would be proud of – he needed to play as if his life depended on it.

Taking his position on the pitch, Marcus caught José's eye. In the dressing room his advice to Marcus had been clear, "Rom will deal with the centre-backs. You stay on the last man and get in behind. Your pace is key for me today."

José's words proved prophetic inside 15 minutes. Lukaku won a header and flicked the ball towards

Marcus, who was already away from Liverpool's teenage full-back Trent Alexander-Arnold.

Marcus raced into the box and, just as Alexander-Arnold caught up with him, he flicked the ball between the defender's legs, cutting back in and then onto his right foot.

Marcus then whipped the ball with his right foot, crashing it towards the far corner, the one that his research had told him was least favoured by the goalkeeper, Karius.

GOAL!

It was a goal that meant so much to Marcus, and he wanted to celebrate it with his fellow fans, so he ran over to them just as he'd done for his very first goal with the club. This goal almost meant as much, and he was sure his younger self would have been jumping around his living room with Dwaine.

And then, 10 minutes later, Marcus had his second. Lukaku was at the centre, battling with Liverpool's centre-backs, when he fed the ball towards Juan Mata. It was poked clear, but only as far as Marcus.

Marcus's research had also shown him that Karius

liked to start high up, so taking a quick shot – again to the far post – wouldn't give the keeper the opportunity to set himself.

So Marcus slammed it in quickly.

GOAL!

Marcus simply raised his arms in the air and started walking toward the crowd.

Liverpool pulled a goal back in the second half and continued to be dominant on the ball. But Marcus always felt that United were the more dangerous of the two.

He certainly didn't want to come off when José summoned him after 70 minutes, but the manager had a good reason.

"I wouldn't have subbed you, Marcus, but I want you fresh for the Champions League game on Tuesday," José said.

Marcus smiled and felt a swell of pride that he'd worked his way up to being the kind of player that José wanted to rest for the big matches.

"Listen to the crowd," José suddenly added, looking up into the stands.

Marcus closed his eyes and listened – they were booing. They didn't want Marcus taken off – they wanted him on the pitch, and José was loving it.

"You're a hero round here, Marcus," he said, clapping him on the back.

19
RASHFORD IN RUSSIA

July 2018 World Cup, Spartak Stadium, Moscow, Russia
England v Columbia

It didn't take Marcus long to fall in love with being at a World Cup.

There was excitement and anticipation in the air at all times, with fans from every corner of the globe filling the streets with their singing and celebrations – and this time, in Russia, England's fans were some of the loudest.

They certainly had good reason to be. The England

team were playing well – better than they'd done in decades, and Marcus was thrilled to be in Russia, playing a small part in it.

A summer away from Manchester also couldn't have come at a better time, as the atmosphere at Man United had become rather toxic. They had finished in second place in the league, but were a mammoth 19 points adrift of runaway leaders Man City – and they had been beaten by Chelsea in the FA Cup Final.

It was now clear that seasons without trophies did not suit José. He was losing his temper more often, was more critical in training and when speaking with the press, as well as openly questioning the attitudes and work ethic of several players.

Marcus had already learnt not to let it affect him, and he'd actually finished the year with his best goals tally so far. He knew he needed to bring the same sense of calm with him to the match today – a last-16 tie with Colombia.

The game was a bad-tempered affair, and Marcus watched from the bench as Harry Kane gave England the lead, followed by a last-minute Colombia equaliser that forced the game into extra time.

Marcus was brought on in the middle of extra time. He was fresh and was able to find opportunities against the tiring Colombian defence, but his England team-mates were equally exhausted and together they struggled to make the most of it.

It was soon obvious that the game would end up with a penalty shootout – something that England had never won at a World Cup.

At the end of 120 minutes Marcus was one of the few England players with any energy left, so he took the responsibility of the second penalty, straight after Kane.

He showed no emotion as Falcao scored for Colombia, then Harry scored for England, and Cuadrado scored for Colombia.

Now it was his turn, and missing wasn't an option.

It was a long walk up to the penalty spot, and he took the time to clear his mind and take all the pressure away. It was just him, a ball, and a goal – no different from how it had been all those years ago, at home in his back garden.

When the whistle went he just side-stepped around the edge of the box, sprinted forward and slammed the ball into the left-hand corner.

GOAL!

Seeing the ball ripple the back of the net was an incredible sight. He'd delivered for his country in its hour of need, and now he just had to pray that the other lads did the same.

The first person to miss was Jordan Henderson, so advantage Colombia. But then Jordan Pickford pulled off a miracle, and it all came down to Eric Dier.

Together with everybody in the stadium – and countless millions around the world – Marcus held his breath.

GOAL!

England were into the quarter finals! The nation's dream wasn't over!

Marcus ran around on the pitch, grabbing and hugging all his team-mates, reeling at the fact he, Marcus Rashford, from Wythenshawe, Manchester, was a member of the first England squad to win a penalty shootout at a World Cup! This was a high like no other.

But this high was soon followed by a low like no other, as England were knocked out of the competition in the semi-finals by Croatia.

At the end of the Croatia match, while watching the opposition team celebrating, Marcus found it difficult to deal emotionally with the disappointment. After all the effort they'd put in, and after getting so far in this tournament, England would not be bringing the trophy home.

Then Marcus started to be critical of his own performance. He was annoyed that he'd only been good enough to be used sparingly. And he was annoyed that he'd not scored any goals, apart from that penalty.

But words of reassurance from his team-mates, who were all consoling each other on the pitch, helped him get things into perspective.

"Four years. We're a young squad. We'll still be in our prime next time around."

Hearing that, Marcus stiffened his resolve. This team had gained the nation's respect. Now they needed to bring an international trophy home, and he was going to keep his head down and become the great player that would help them do it.

But he wasn't going to wait four years to do it. The 2020 Euros were going to be *his* tournament.

20
OLE AT THE WHEEL

December 2018, Manchester United training ground
Manchester, England

When Marcus heard that José had been sacked mid-season he wasn't hugely surprised. Even before Christmas, United were already effectively out of two competitions.

Nevertheless, Marcus was a little sad to see him go. For all the difficulties he'd faced under José, the man had taught him tactical awareness and positioning to a degree that he wouldn't have learned from any other manager.

And he knew that he'd learned from his 'difficulties' with José too. They had helped steel him for whatever might come his way in the future – including the next United manager, whoever it might be. And some of the biggest names across Europe were being touted for the job.

"I'm telling you, it's going to be Mauricio Pochettino," Jesse had said confidently when the players were discussing it in the canteen.

"No, I heard it's Ancelotti or Allegri," Chris Smalling had replied.

But in the end United decided to go with someone a littler closer to home – they were bringing in United legend and former player, Ole Gunnar Solskjær.

And now, in the first team meeting of the season, Marcus was excited to see that Ole had a very different manner to José's. With a huge smile on his face, Ole looked genuinely excited to be meeting everyone.

There were also no rambling speeches about winning the league – Ole was grounded and to the point.

"At the moment we're not playing like Manchester United," he said simply. "That's what we need to get back to. High pressing, hard running, getting the ball to our strikers quickly ... "

He looked around the room, gauging the player's reactions to what he was saying, and Marcus could sense that, while he might *seem* a soft touch, beneath the surface was a man who was determined to win. Ole had scored more than 100 goals for United in his playing career, and you didn't achieve that if you were soft.

The training sessions that followed focused on running and quick passing, but halfway through Ole pulled Marcus and a couple of the other strikers aside.

"You guys are my strikers," he said, "and I want to get you clinical."

Hearing that he was once again going to be used as a striker made Marcus's heart soar. He'd learnt to handle playing on the wing, but being a striker was the position he'd dreamt of playing for United ever since seeing Ronaldo play at Old Trafford – a match that Ole had played in himself.

The manager then began to set up a few drills, and

it was obvious that he'd been a top level player, taking a much more hands-on approach that Marcus loved.

"Marcus!" he shouted after one drill. "Guide the ball into the goal, don't snatch at it. Look, like this."

Then they worked on the importance of eye contact with the keeper …

Then they worked on how to time runs into the box …

And then they worked on what to do when the ball was out wide …

By the time the session was over, Marcus could feel the training ground had been charged with a new kind of energy. He could see that the other players had responded in the same way.

He was excited to see what Ole would do for this club – and what he would do for him.

21
THE THEATRE OF DREAMS

July 2020, Old Trafford, Manchester
Manchester United v Bournemouth

As he walked from the dressing room to the Old Trafford tunnel, Marcus reflected on how lucky he'd been when it came to injuries.

It was other players' injuries that had opened the doors to United's first team for him, gifting him his chance to walk down this tunnel for the first time at the tender age of eighteen.

And now, after picking up an injury of his own last January, he'd been 'lucky' in that something unprecedented had happened. The world of professional football had ground to a halt because of a virus. There had been no football for three months, which had given Marcus time to recover.

Now professional football had restarted in the UK, but matches were being played in empty stadiums, owing to the continuing pandemic.

So now, Marcus was walking on to the pitch for a match against Bournemouth – and an important milestone was within reach.

After a full season of scoring under Ole, as part of a dangerous front-three, Marcus was now one goal away from getting 20 goals for the season.

He smiled at the thought.

When he was growing up he'd always thought that getting 20 goals in a season was the sign of a world-class striker. After all, it was what he'd blurted out when Mourinho had asked him, in their first meeting in his office, what he'd wanted to achieve.

Back then, Marcus had had one good half-season

under his belt and had been terrified of the man in front of him. Now he'd played almost four and a half seasons, and he wasn't going to let anything prevent him from making his dreams a reality.

The whistle went – and the game got off to the worst possible start for Man United.

Bournemouth were in the middle of a relegation battle at the bottom of the league so, with nothing to lose, they pulled out all the stops.

After just 15 minutes, Junior Stanislas dribbled his way into the box and was able to scoop the ball past de Gea to score.

Bournemouth had the lead.

But this was a new era of a confident, attacking United, and they were unfazed by this setback.

About 14 minutes later, Man U levelled, with a powerful shot, slammed past the keeper and into the back of the net.

"We can do this, lads!" Marcus shouted to his team-mates, as they celebrated the goal. "Now let's keep up the pressure and get another!"

The game quickly restarted and, moments later, the

ball bounced off the hand of one of the Bournemouth players. Immediately the ref pointed to the spot.

Marcus was quick to step up.

He could still remember his first professional penalty for United, against PSG in the Champions League. He'd showed such fearlessness that he'd become one of the club's first-choice penalty takers, and now he was going to remind everyone why he deserved that role.

Sure enough, he struck the ball cleanly and sweetly, and it slammed into the bottom right-hand corner. The keeper stood no chance.

GOAL!

It was his 20th of the season – with more games still left to play.

Marcus took a moment to look around his beloved stadium, 'The Theatre of Dreams'. Even though the stands were empty, it was still a magnificent sight – as wonderful now as the first time he'd come here with Dwaine all those years ago.

United eventually ran out 5-2 winners against Bournemouth, helping them take a huge step towards Champions League football next season.

Marcus walked off the pitch feeling proud. He was part of a United team that now truly felt like the teams he'd watched when he'd been growing up – the teams that had won every trophy in the game.

He was also part of the best England squad in a generation, a squad that would have another chance to prove itself at the Euros next year.

And he was on his way to becoming one of the most lethal strikers in the game.

22

HELPING OUT

October 2020, Old Trafford, Manchester
Manchester United v RB Leipzig

As Marcus walked off the pitch, he felt a swell of emotions swirling around in his mind.

Thrashing Leipzig 5-0 had left him feeling lightheaded – and it wasn't until he was half-way down the tunnel that he could truly appreciate the fact that he'd scored three of those goals in just 16 minutes.

It was his first senior hat-trick.

His achievement was made even more impressive by the events of the last few months.

The continuing pandemic was still wreaking havoc on professional football. This year there hadn't been a proper summer break – and many clubs were worried about the impact that might have on players' fitness and mental well-being.

But clearly it wasn't proving to be a problem for Marcus. In fact, as he walked down the tunnel, he knew that he was playing some of the best football of his life.

And he was achieving a whole lot more off the pitch as well.

A few months back, after hearing about the ways this pandemic was pushing many families into serious hardship, memories of his own childhood had played out before his eyes – of the conversations he'd often had with his mum about struggling to afford food for her kids.

It wasn't a conversation that he wanted any other families to be having.

So he'd used his voice to persuade the government to provide vouchers for vulnerable families to spend on food.

He'd even been awarded an MBE ('Member of the British Empire') by the UK government for these charitable efforts. Outside of football, an MBE is one of the most prestigious awards a person can receive.

And now, as he turned into the dressing room and was met with a cheer from the coaching staff and players already there, a determined smile spread across Marcus's face.

He felt stronger than ever, as if he could handle anything both on and off the pitch.

He was making a difference. And he was ready for whatever would come next.

23
JUST GETTING STARTED

February 2023, Wembley Stadium, London, England
2023 League Cup Final, Man United v Newcastle

Marcus bent down and swept a hand over the Wembley turf. He was relieved to be back here, playing in another final. This time, it was the League Cup final against Newcastle.

"It's kind of an intimidating atmosphere, right?" Luke Shaw remarked, nodding in the direction of the Newcastle fans, who were making the most of the occasion.

"We played at the Nou Camp barely two weeks ago," Marcus grinned. "It's nothing compared to that. And we're at Wembley all the time – we're used to this kind of atmosphere."

He took a moment to gaze around the stadium properly – a stadium that was now so familiar to him.

Wembley had played host to some of the greatest moments of his career. He'd triumphed here in the 2016 FA Cup final, and had scored a brilliant winning goal against Spurs in the Premier League. And then there were the many important goals he'd scored for England …

But he'd also suffered some of his lowest moments at Wembley. He'd lost the semi-final of the 2020 FA Cup to Chelsea here. And had experienced his lowest moment for England – when he'd lost the final of Euro 2020 to Italy.

Marcus grimaced as he glanced over to the penalty area where it had all gone so wrong for England in that game. Three England players had missed in the penalty shootout, and Marcus had been one of them

"That was a bad day," Luke said, reading his mind.

"At least you scored," Marcus replied. "I've just got bad memories."

Luke had scored the opening goal in the final – after just two minutes. The game had ultimately finished 1-1, after Bonucci had equalised, and had gone all the way to penalties. Marcus had been third up for England.

He'd bravely stepped up, and had struck his penalty well. The keeper couldn't get close to it – but he hadn't needed to. The ball had cannoned back off the post. Marcus had missed.

After his miss, England had missed their next two penalties – losing the shootout 3-2.

The months that had followed were some of the worst of Marcus's career. He'd been plagued by injuries, criticism in the media, and poor form.

There'd been changes at Man U too. Their manager, Ole Gunnar Solskjær, had been sacked, replaced by Ralf Rangnick. There were new faces at the club in the form of Jadon Sancho, Raphaël Varane, and one of Marcus's childhood heroes – Cristiano Ronaldo. Marcus had had to pinch himself every time he took to the pitch with his idol.

But the fairytale had come to a disappointing end.

As soon as he'd arrived, Cristiano had departed, dropped by the new United manager, Erik ten Hag, who'd in turn replaced Ralf Rangnick.

In place of Ronaldo, ten Hag had turned to Marcus to be the central focus of his team. The new manager believed in playing an energetic high-press system, and Marcus's natural work rate and pace made him the perfect fit for United's new-look front-three.

After ten Hag's first few games, the prospects of a cup final and a place in the top four of the Premier League had seemed unlikely. United had been battered by both Brentford and Brighton, as they'd struggled to adapt to their manager's style of play.

But then Marcus had found an extra gear. He'd scored in statement wins against Liverpool and Arsenal, and then, after England's disappointing World Cup in Qatar, he'd taken it up another level.

He was one of the top scorers in Europe in 2023. He'd scored at the Nou Camp against Barcelona, he'd scored the winner in the Manchester derby – and he'd been on fire at the World Cup, where he'd scored three goals.

The worst year of his career had made way for the best form of his life. He felt as if he was going to score every time he took to the pitch.

And now, he finally had a shot at a trophy.

United hadn't won a trophy since winning the 2017 Europa League and, for a club of their stature, six years was a massive drought.

But today, they were playing Newcastle in the League Cup final.

Marcus was lining up on the left wing for the game. This was his preferred role – allowing him the freedom to make deep runs behind the defence, knowing he had Luke for cover behind him.

United now also had the imposing presence of Wout Weghorst up front. He would keep the Newcastle defenders busy, while Marcus got in behind them.

"It'll be tough against Kieran today," Luke added, gesturing to their England team-mate, the Newcastle captain, Kieran Trippier.

He'd been one of the best defenders in the league this

season, and Newcastle had been one of the best teams in the league. They were battling United for a place in the top four.

But United were a vastly improved side from last year. The club had made important new signings in the form of Casemiro, Eriksen and Lisandro Martínez.

The team were in brilliant form and were now completely in sync with ten Hag's style of play. He'd built a team to win trophies – and today was their chance to prove it.

Marcus knew how important it would be to silence the vocal Newcastle crowd. An early goal would do that.

It took until the 31st minute for United to get the breakthrough. Luke fizzed in a cross from the left, and Casemiro met it with a bullet header into the back of the net.

And then, Marcus got his chance. A clever pass from Weghorst sent him running in behind the Newcastle backline. His first touch took him clear of their desperate grasps, and his second touch fired away a powerful shot.

A year ago it might have deflected wide, or been a

scuffed effort. But Marcus was not the same player he was a year ago. The ball deflected off the final Newcastle defender and looped into the back of the net.

It was Marcus's first goal in a cup final. He'd put United 2-0 up, and he knew there was no way his team would loosen their grip on the trophy now.

Newcastle huffed and puffed, but they never came close to getting back into the game.

Marcus was subbed off with just two minutes remaining, and he soaked in the adulation of the United fans as he made his way off. His job was done.

A couple of years ago, he'd scored 20 goals in his best-scoring season. It had been a massive achievement at the time.

Today's goal was his 25th of the season. He was closing in on 30, and would no doubt get there before the end of the season.

But, more than that, this was his first trophy in a long time.

He felt more optimistic about United than ever, and was excited about where the club was heading. He hadn't felt like that for many years.

At just 25 years old, he'd become the man United looked to. And now, he had an opportunity to write himself into their record books.

Last year, it had seemed as if the Marcus Rashford story might be faltering. But now, it was only just getting started.